EVIL MONKEY MEMES!
BY N BLAKE SEALS
ARTWORK BY BUTCH MAPA & MAURICIO LEONE

EDITED BY VINCENT FERRANTE
DESIGN AND EDITORIAL PRODUCTION BY BLAKE

EVIL MONKEY MEMES! PUBLISHED BY MONARCH COMICS.
©2021 MONARCH COMICS, LLC./EMM HOLDINGS, INC. ALL RIGHTS RESERVED.
NO PART OF THIS PUBLICATION MAY BE REPRODUCED OR TRANSMITTED IN ANY FORM OR BY
ANY MEANS, EXCEPT SHORT EXCERPTS FOR REVIEW, WITHOUT THE EXPRESS WRITTEN
PERMISSION OF THE AUTHOR OR PUBLISHER.

WWW.MONARCHCOMICS.COM

EVIL MONKEY MAN!
IT WAS A SONG. THEN IT WAS A COMIC BOOK. NOW...IT'S A MEME.
ISN'T EVERYTHING?
THE HALLMARK OF TWENTY FIRST CENTURY INSTAGRAM PHILOSOPHY.
THE MEME.

INITIALLY A BY-PRODUCT OF PROMOTING THE COMIC, THESE MEME'S, CREATED FOR FACEBOOK, EVENTUALLY TOOK ON A LIFE OF THEIR OWN, AND WITH TENS OF THOUSANDS OF LIKES AND SHARES, DESERVE A BOOK OF THEIR OWN - EVEN IF IT IS A REALLY LITTLE BOOK. ONE YOU CAN LEAVE IN THE BATHROOM FOR COMMODIOUS ENJOYMENT ;)

SO THEN, IN THE TRADITION OF THE ONE-LINER, THE IRREVERANT SARCASM OF THE GOTCHA, AND THE ELEVATED ART OF THE COFFEE TABLE JOKE BOOK...PLEASE ENJOY THIS, THE VERY FIRST COLLECTION OF *EVIL MONKEY MEMES..!*

ART · BUTCH MAPA · EMM EPISODE TWO

ART · BUTCH MAPA · EMM EPISODE TWO

ART • BUTCH MAPA • EMM EPISODE THREE

ART · BUTCH MAPA · EMM EPISODE ONE

ART · BUTCH MAPA · EMM EPISODE TWO

ART · BUTCH MAPA · EMM EPISODE ONE & TWO

ART • BUTCH MAPA • EMM EPISODE ONE

ART • BUTCH MAPA • EMM EPISODE TWO

ART · BUTCH MAPA · EMM EPISODE ONE

ART · BUTCH MAPA · EMM EPISODE TWO

ART · BUTCH MAPA · EMM EPISODE ONE

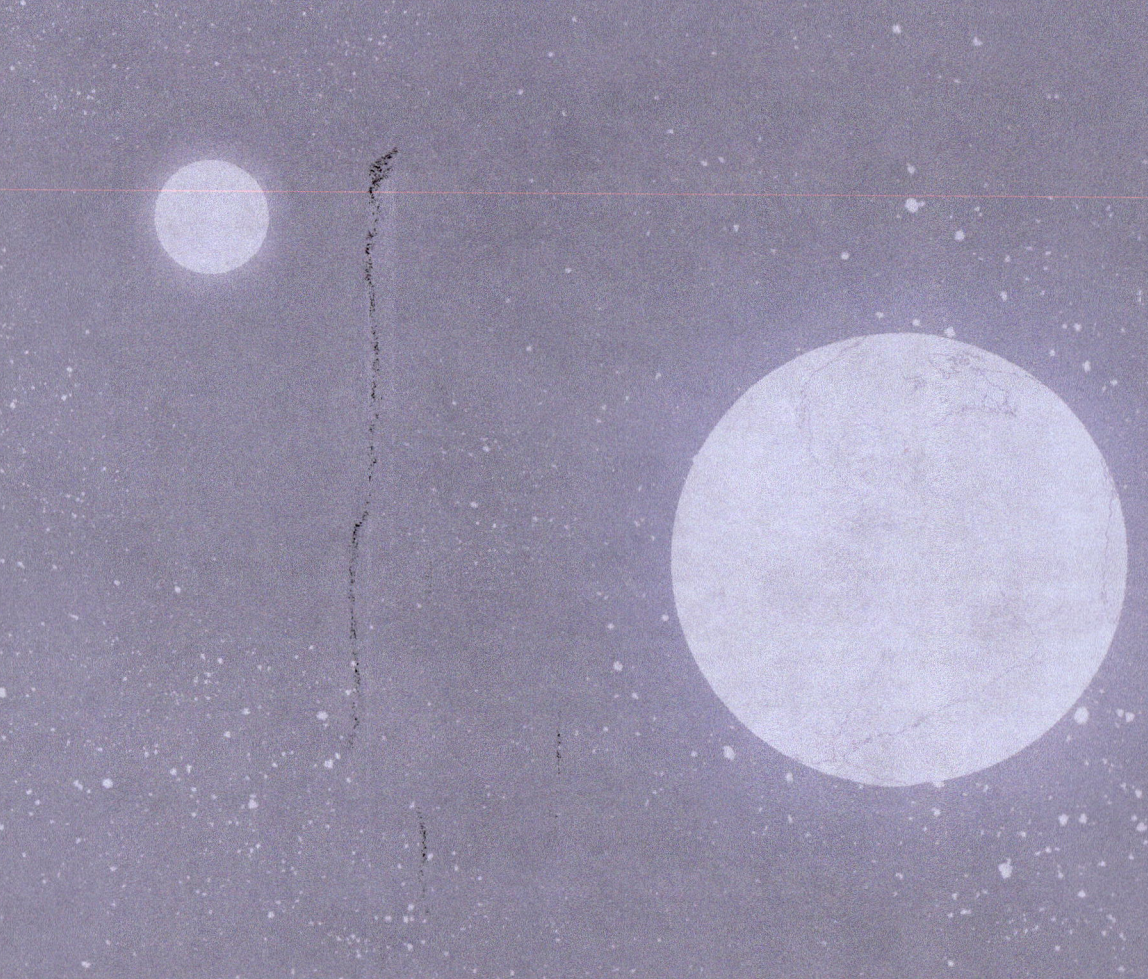

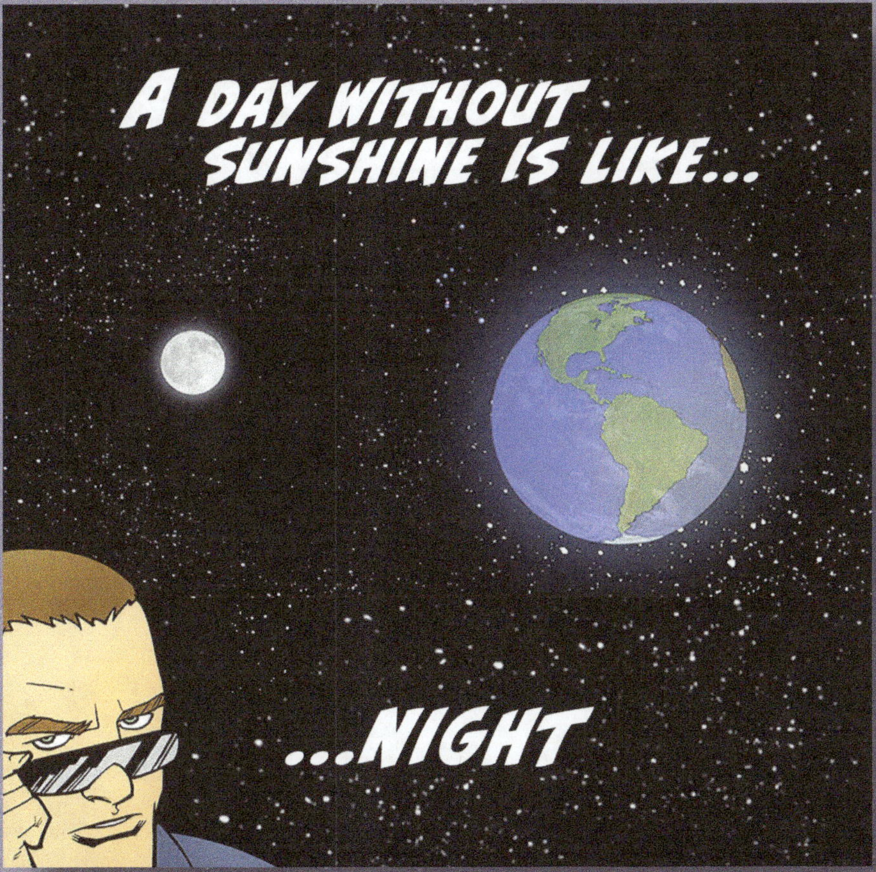
A DAY WITHOUT SUNSHINE IS LIKE...
...NIGHT

ART · BUTCH MAPA · EMM EPISODES TWO & THREE

ART · BUTCH MAPA · EMM EPISODE THREE

ART · BUTCH MAPA · EMM EPISODE THREE

ART · BUTCH MAPA · EMM EPISODE TWO

ART · BUTCH MAPA · EMM EPISODE THREE

ART · BUTCH MAPA · EMM EPISODE TWO

ART · BUTCH MAPA · EMM EPISODE THREE

ART · MAURICIO LEONE · EMM EPISODE FIVE

ART · BUTCH MAPA · EMM EPISODE TWO

ART · BUTCH MAPA · EMM EPISODE THREE

ART · BUTCH MAPA · EMM EPISODE FOUR

ART · BUTCH MAPA · EMM EPISODE FOUR

ART · BUTCH MAPA · EMM EPISODE TWO

ART · BUTCH MAPA · EMM EPISODE TWO

ART · BUTCH MAPA · EMM EPISODE TWO

ART · BUTCH MAPA · EMM EPISODE FOUR

ART · BUTCH MAPA · EMM EPISODE THREE

ART · MAURICIO LEONE · EMM EPISODE FIVE

ART · BUTCH MAPA · EMM EPISODE FOUR

ART • BUTCH MAPA • EMM EPISODE ONE

ART · BUTCH MAPA · EMM EPISODE TWO

ART · BUTCH MAPA · EMM EPISODE FOUR

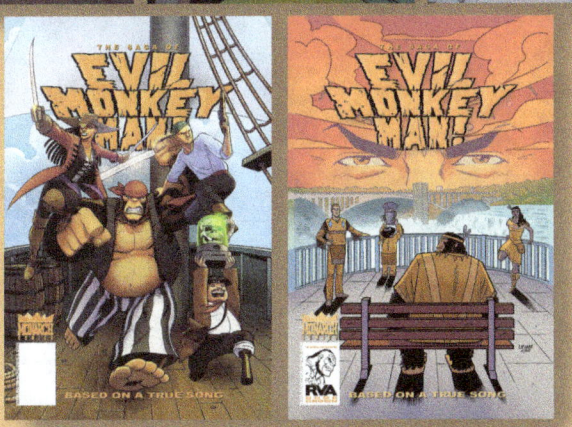

FEATURING ARTWORK BY BUTCH MAPA & MAURICIO LEONE
FROM THE SAGA OF EVIL MONKEY MAN!
EPISODES 1 - 5
AVAILABLE AT WWW.MONARCHCOMICS.COM

THE AWARD WINNING GRAPHIC NOVEL

THE SAGA OF EVIL MONKEY MAN! SEASON ONE
BY N BLAKE SEALS & BUTCH MAPA

AVAILABLE NOW
WWW.MONARCHCOMICS.COM
AND AT FINE BOOK & COMIC BOOK STORES WORLDWIDE
INCLUDING AMAZON.COM & BARNESANDNOBEL.COM

    THE PEACEFUL SERENITY OF NEW YORK SUBURB COLD SPRING HARBOR IS JOLTED WITH AN INEXPLICABLE EXPLOSION. AS FIREFIGHTERS RACE INTO BATTLE THERE ARE NOW REPORTS OF SOME SORT OF TALKING APE-MAN RUNNING AROUND TOWN.
    IT'S A MIND-ALTERING, TIME-TRAVELING, REALITY-BENDING, CRISS-CROSS QUEST ACROSS AMERICA IN A SEARCH FOR A WAY TO BECOME HUMAN ONCE AGAIN.
    JOIN MIKE, THE MONKEY MAN, LINA, THE KUNG-FU CHICK, MANNY, THE MUTE MIDGET, MENKE MOON, THE MAD SCIENTIST, AND DOC, THE CRUSTY NAVY CORPSMAN, AS THEY FIND THEIR WAY TO HERE THERE AND EVERYWHERE, ALL WHILE BEING PURSUED BY SOME SHADY FEDERAL AGENTS.
    IT'S ALL FUN AND GAMES - UNTIL SOMEONE GETS TURNED INTO A MONKEY!
    COLLECTS ISSUES 1-4 OF THE POPULAR INDIE COMIC BOOK *THE SAGA OF EVIL MONKEY MAN!* WRITTEN BY N BLAKE SEALS, ART BY BUTCH MAPA WITH COLOR BY BLAKE. COVER BY BUTCH MAPA WITH COLOR BY K MICHAEL RUSSELL.

AN IBPA BENJAMIN FRANKLIN AWARD WINNER
AND READERS' FAVORITE FIVE STAR SELECTION.

"AN ENTERTAINING, COLORFUL ADVENTURE WITH A STRIKING HERO. SEALS' BREEZY NOVEL...IS MADCAP FUN. MAPA'S ARTWORK IS PRISTINE."
   -*KIRKUS REVIEWS*

"IT'S FUN, FUNNY, OR BOTH. EXCELLENT ENTERTAINMENT."
   -*JIM SHOOTER - LEGENDARY EDITOR-IN CHIEF OF MARVEL & VALIANT COMICS*

"THE SAGA OF EVIL MONKEY MAN: SEASON ONE IS MARVELOUS, SPECTACULAR AND SO MUCH FUN TO READ. IT'S BEAUTIFULLY PUT TOGETHER: THE ART, COLORING, STORYLINE, AND THE RESULT IS A PROFESSIONALLY DESIGNED AND CREATED STORY THAT'S WACKY, ENTERTAINING, AND FILLED WITH FAST-PACED ACTION. SEALS' CHARACTERS ARE WELL-CRAFTED, AND HIS PLOT IS INGENIOUS AND CLEVER."
   -*JACK MAGNUS FOR READERS' FAVORITE*

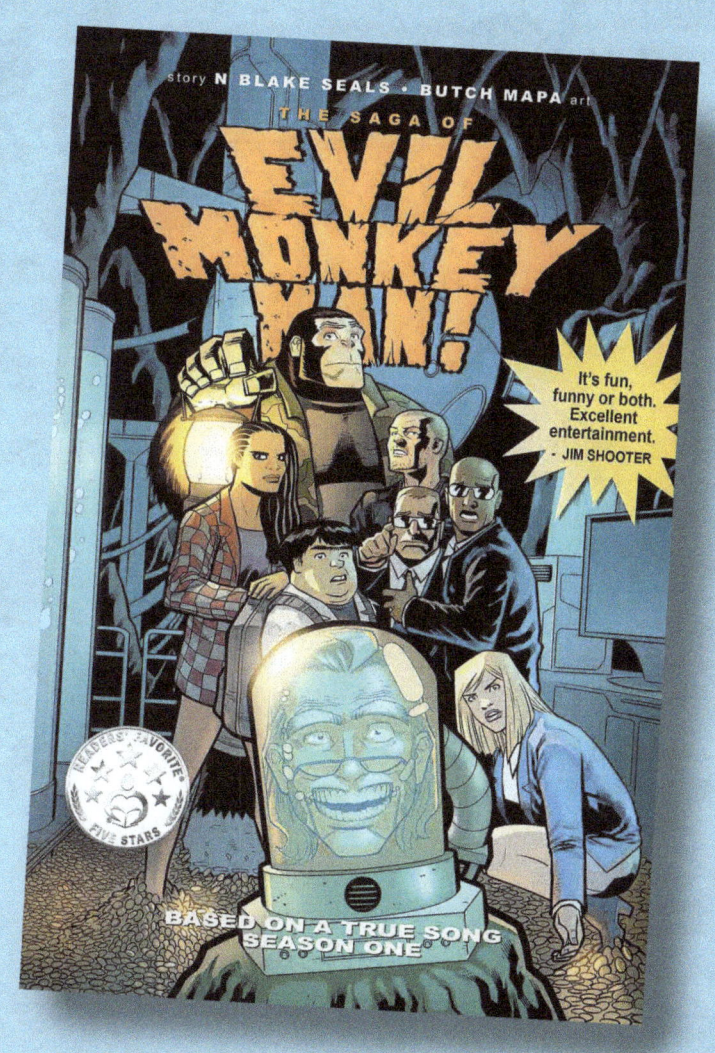

www.ingramcontent.com/pod-product-compliance
Lightning Source LLC
Chambersburg PA
CBHW081419080526
44589CB00016B/2606